FOOD LOVERS

SALSAS, DRESSINGS & SAUCES

FOOD LOVERS

SALSAS, DRESSINGS & SAUCES

RECIPES SELECTED BY RENE CHAN

Trans
Atlantic
Press

CONTENTS

CREAMY HERB SAUCE

Ingredients

4 tbsp / 50 g butter

½ cup / 50 g flour

2 cups / 500 ml vegetable broth (stock)

2 tbsp chopped fresh chervil

2 tbsp chopped chives

1 tbsp chopped fresh parsley

1 tbsp chopped fresh dill

¼ cup / 50 ml sour cream

Salt and freshly ground pepper

1 scallion (spring onion)

Chives, for garnishing

Method

Prep and cook time: 25 min

1 Melt the butter in a skillet (fying pan). Add the flour, whisking constantly until the flour begins to color.

2 Gradually add the broth (stock) while whisking constantly. Continue whisking and simmer over a low heat for 15 minutes. Remove the sauce from the heat.

3 Add the chervil, chives, parsley, and dill. Mix briefly with a hand-held mixer.

4 Stir in the sour cream and season with salt and pepper.

5 Slice the scallions (spring onions) into thin rings. Fill a small bowl with the sauce. Sprinkle with the scallion rings and garnish with the chives. The sauce makes a wonderful accompaniment for roasted meat, poached fish or steamed vegetables.

FRENCH DRESSING

Ingredients

1 small shallot, very finely chopped

1 tbsp white wine vinegar

¾ tsp Dijon mustard

Plenty of freshly ground black pepper

6 tbsp extra virgin olive oil

Sprinkle of sea salt (optional)

Method

Prep and cook time: 5 min

Put all the ingredients in a jar and shake until well emulsified.

For a milder version

- Omit the mustard or use less
- Use white pepper instead of black pepper
- Use vegetable oil or a milder tasting olive oil

For an Asian feel

- Substitute ½ tsp of olive oil for sesame or chili oil
- Substitute rice vinegar for white wine vinegar

Orange version – perfect with spinach salads

- Add 1 tbsp runny honey
- Add the juice and zest of 1 large orange
- Use balsamic instead of white wine vinegar

GARLIC MAYONNAISE

Ingredients

5 large garlic cloves

3 egg yolks

1 tsp hot mustard

White pepper

1¼ cups / 300 ml olive oil

½ tbsp lemon juice

Salt

Method

Prep and cook time: 15 min

1 Peel and crush the garlic cloves.

2 Combine the egg yolks, garlic, mustard and a pinch of salt and pepper in a large bowl. Beat until creamy.

3 Add the oil, drop by drop (later in a slow stream) beating constantly. Incorporate the oil completely into the mixture before adding more. When the oil is fully incorporated, stir in the lemon juice.

4 Season with salt and pepper to taste and serve.

SUN-DRIED TOMATO PESTO

Ingredients

4 oz / 100 g dried tomatoes

½ cup / 50 g pine nuts

2 garlic cloves

Generous ½ cup / 50 g freshly grated Parmesan cheese

About ⅔ cup / 150 ml olive oil

Salt

Cayenne pepper

Method

Prep and cook time: 10 min plus approx 2 hours soaking time

1 Pour boiling water over the tomatoes and let them sit for about 2 hours to rehydrate. Drain well and coarsely chop.

2 Put the tomatoes, pine nuts, peeled garlic and Parmesan cheese in a food processor and chop coarsely.

3 Add the oil in a stream until a creamy pesto forms. Season to taste with salt and cayenne pepper.

WHITE BEAN PURÉE

Ingredients

1¼ cup / 250 g dried lima or haricot (butter or navy) beans, soaked overnight

1 onion

2 garlic cloves

4 tbsp olive oil

2 cups / 500 ml chicken broth (stock)

4 sprigs thyme

2 tbsp crème fraîche

Salt and freshly ground black pepper

Method

Prep and cook time: 1 hour
plus 12 hours soaking time

1 Peel and finely chop the onion and garlic.

2 Heat 1 tbsp olive oil in a large pan and cook the onion and garlic until translucent.

3 Add the broth (stock), the drained beans and 3 thyme sprigs to the pan. Cook until the beans are soft, stirring occasionally (about 45 minutes).

4 Drain the beans, reserving the cooking broth.

5 Remove the thyme sprigs from the beans and purée the mixture until smooth.

6 Stir in the crème fraîche, 2 tbsp of oil and enough broth to form a creamy purée.

7 Season with salt and pepper to taste. Drizzle the remaining olive oil over the top. Garnish with the remaining thyme leaves.

GREEN MELON SALSA

Ingredients

1 Galia melon

1 lime

2 tbsp sugar

$^2/_3$ cup / 150 ml water

1 jalepeno pepper, deseeded and sliced into rings

1 red chili pepper, deseeded and finely chopped

1 tbsp fresh, chopped basil

Method

Prep and cook time: 15 min

1 Slice the melon in half. Remove the seeds, peel and finely dice.

2 Remove the zest from the lime and squeeze out the juice. Put the lime juice, zest, sugar and the water in a saucepan. Bring to a boil and simmer for 4-5 minutes.

3 Add the jalepeno and chili peppers and the basil.

4 Pour the sauce over the diced melon. Mix well and allow to cool.

PEANUT SAUCE

Ingredients

1 cup / 150 g unsalted, shelled peanuts

Generous ¾ cup / 200 ml coconut milk

2 tbsp peanut butter

½ tsp curry powder

Soy sauce

Fish sauce

Method

Prep and cook time: 20 min

1 Toast the peanuts in a dry pan, let cool and finely crush in a mortar.

2 Bring the coconut milk, peanut butter and curry powder to a boil in a saucepan. Stir in the crushed peanuts. Simmer, stirring occasionally, for 5 minutes until creamy.

3 Season to taste with the soy sauce and fish sauce. Allow to cool.

PUMPKIN AND ORANGE CHUTNEY

Ingredients

For 3 x 2-cup / 500 ml jars

2 lb / 800 g pumpkin flesh, rind and seeds removed

4 oranges

2 onions

2 red chili peppers

Generous ¾ cup / 200 ml apple vinegar

2 cloves

2 star anise

²/₃ cup / 150 g sugar

1 tsp salt

1 cup / 250 ml water

Method

Prep and cook time: 1 hour

1 Finely chop the pumpkin flesh.

2 Peel the oranges and coarsely chop the flesh.

3 Peel and chop the onions.

4 Remove the stems of the chile peppers and slice into rings.

5 Bring the pumpkin, onions, chilis, vinegar, cloves, star anise, sugar, salt and the water to a boil. Lower the heat and simmer, stirring occasionally for about 40 minutes.

6 Stir in the oranges and cook for an additional 5 minutes.

7 Fill the prepared jars* with the chutney. Close tightly and allow to cool.

* To prepare the jars: Wash and rinse the jars thoroughly with hot water then place in a roasting pan in a 350° F (180° C/ Gas Mark 4) oven for 5 minutes to sterilize. Fill the jars while they are still hot.

CHILI AND CORIANDER VINAIGRETTE

Ingredients

1 red chili pepper

1 green chili pepper

½ cup / 10 g rau ram or cilantro (fresh coriander) leaves

½ cup / 10 g fresh Thai basil

2 garlic cloves, peeled

8 tsp / 40 ml rice vinegar

2 tbsp soy sauce

⅓ cup / 75 ml vegetable oil

Salt

Method

Prep and cook time: 10 min

1 Rinse and slice the chilis in half, lengthwise. Remove the ribs and seeds.

2 Put the chilis, cilantro (coriander), basil, garlic cloves, vinegar, soy sauce and half of the oil in a food processor and make a fine purée.

3 Mix in the remaining oil and season with salt to taste.

HOLLANDAISE SAUCE

Ingredients

1 tbsp white wine vinegar

½ cup / 125 ml dry white wine

3 egg yolks

2 sticks / 250 g butter

Lemon juice

Salt

Method

Prep and cook time: 20 min

1 Put the vinegar and wine in a small saucepan and reduce by half. Allow to cool.

2 Melt the butter over medium heat. Set aside.

3 Add the reduced liquid to the egg yolks. Whisk in a metal bowl placed over a pan of gently simmering water until creamy.

4 Add the butter drop by drop, whisking continuously. As the sauce thickens you can begin to add the butter in a thin steady stream.

5 Season to taste with the lemon juice and salt.

SWEET AND SOUR CHILI SAUCE

Ingredients

For 2 x 14 fl oz / 400 ml bottles

10 red chili peppers

1 onion

5 cloves garlic

7 tbsp / 100 ml apple vinegar

1 tbsp salt

¾ cup / 150 g brown sugar

2 cups / 500 ml water

Method

Prep and cook time: 40 min

1 Rinse the chili peppers and remove the stem. Peel the onion and garlic and coarsely chop.

2 Put the chili, onion and garlic in a food processor and finely chop.

3 Put the finely chopped vegetables in a pan together with the apple vinegar, salt, sugar and the water and bring to a boil. Simmer, stirring occasionally, for about 30 minutes until the sauce thickens.

4 Pour the sauce into prepared bottles*, close tightly and allow to cool.

∗ To prepare the bottles: Wash and rinse the bottles thoroughly with hot water then place in a roasting pan in a 350° F (180° C/ Gas Mark 4) oven for 5 minutes to sterilize. Fill the bottles while they are still hot.

BÉARNAISE SAUCE

Ingredients

About 1 cup / 200 g butter

2 shallots

10 tsp / 50 ml dry white wine

10 tsp / 50 ml white wine vinegar

3 egg yolks

1 tbsp chopped fresh tarragon leaves

1 tbsp chopped fresh chervil leaves

Salt

Freshly ground, white pepper

Method

Prep and cook time: 30 min

1 Melt the butter and skim off the foam.

2 Peel and finely chop the shallots.

3 Put the shallots, wine and vinegar in a small saucepan. Reduce by half over medium heat (about 10 minutes). Allow to cool completely. Strain the mixture through a sieve.

4 Add the strained liquid to the egg yolks and beat the mixture until the consistency is creamy.

5 Place the bowl over a pan of gently simmering water and add the butter, drop by drop to start with, and then in a thin stream, stirring constantly, until the sauce is creamy and shiny.

6 Stir in the tarragon and chervil. Season to taste with salt and pepper.

RÉMOULADE SAUCE

Ingredients

4 oz / 100 g dill pickles (gerkins),
with 2 tbsp pickling liquid

1 shallot

1 cup / 250 g mayonnaise

2 tbsp fresh, chopped tarragon

2 tbsp fresh, chopped parsley

1 tbsp hot mustard

Lemon juice

Method

Prep and cook time: 15 min

1 Finely chop the pickles.

2 Peel and finely chop the shallot.

3 Mix the pickles, shallot, mayonnaise, the pickling liquid, tarragon, parsley and mustard together until smooth.

4 Season to taste with the lemon juice, salt and pepper.

MANGO SALSA

Ingredients

1 mango, peeled and pit removed

1 pear, peeled and cored

1 red bell pepper

1 red chili pepper

2 scallions (spring onions), sliced into thin rings

1 tbsp chopped mint

1 tbsp chopped cilantro (fresh coriander) leaves

1 lime

1 tsp brown sugar

Salt

Method

Prep and cook time: 40 min

1 Finely dice the mango and pear flesh and place in a dish.

2 Remove the ribs and seeds of the bell pepper and the chili. Finely dice the bell pepper and finely mince the chili pepper.

3 Add the scallions (spring onions), bell pepper, chili pepper and the herbs to the pear-mango mixture.

4 Squeeze the juice from the lime and stir the juice and sugar into the salsa. Allow to marinate for about 30 minutes.

5 Season with salt to taste before serving.

SOUR CREAM DIP

Ingredients

2 garlic cloves

1¼ cups / 300 ml sour cream

Salt and freshly ground black pepper

2 tbsp olive oil

Chives, for garnishing

Method

Prep and cook time: 10 min

1 Peel and finely chop the garlic cloves. Add a pinch of salt.

2 Using the flat side of a knife, crush the garlic into a paste.

3 Mix the garlic paste into the sour cream. Stir until smooth. Season to taste with salt and the pepper.

4 Fill a small bowl with the dip. Sprinkle with pepper and drizzle a little oil over the top. Garnish with chives and serve.

MINTED ONION SAUCE

Ingredients

2 onions

1 garlic clove

2 tbsp vegetable oil

1 tsp sugar

1 cup / 250 ml red wine

2 tbsp red wine vinegar

2 sprigs fresh mint

Salt

Freshly ground pepper

Method

Prep and cook time: 20 min

1 Peel and finely chop the onions and garlic clove and sauté in hot oil for 30 seconds.

2 Sprinkle with the sugar and continue to sauté for another minute until translucent.

3 Pour in the red wine and vinegar.

4 Strip the mint leaves from the stems. Set a few leaves aside for garnishing. Coarsely chop the rest and add to the sauce.

5 Simmer gently for about 10 minutes.

6 Remove from the heat and season with salt and pepper. Allow the sauce to cool to lukewarm.

7 Before serving season to taste with salt and pepper and garnish with the reserved mint leaves.

LEMON BARBECUE SAUCE

Ingredients

2 lemons

2 cups / 40 g fresh parsley

2 tbsp fresh oregano leaves

2 garlic cloves

Generous ¾ cup / 200 ml olive oil

Salt

Method

Prep and cook time: 10 min

1 Remove and finely chop the zest from one lemon.

2 Squeeze the juice from both lemons.

3 Put the lemon juice, zest, parsley leaves, oregano and peeled garlic in a tall container. Purée with a hand-held mixer while adding the oil in a steady stream. Season with salt to taste.

4 Serve with grilled fish or meat.

TOMATO AND GREEN PEPPER SAUCE

Ingredients

2 shallots

2 tbsp green peppercorns

2 tbsp olive oil

7 tbsp / 100 ml dry white wine

1 cup / 200 g canned tomatoes, chopped

4 tbsp crème fraîche

Salt

Method

Prep and cook time: 30 min

1 Peel the shallots and slice thinly.

2 Heat the oil in a pan and sauté the peppercorns for 2 minutes. Add the shallots and continue to sauté for another minute.

3 Pour in the white wine and add the tomatoes. Simmer, stirring occasionally, for about 20 minutes.

4 Stir in the crème fraîche. Season to taste with salt.

HERB AND CHILI MARINADE

Ingredients

3 garlic cloves

1 shallot

2 cups / 40 g chopped fresh herbs – eg rosemary, mint, basil

1 red chili pepper, deseeded and finely chopped

Scant ¼ cup / 50 ml olive oil

1 tsp hot mustard

2 tbsp white balsamic vinegar

Salt and pepper

Method

Prep and cook time: 10 min

1 Peel and finely chop the garlic cloves and shallot.

2 Combine the garlic, shallots, chili pepper and herbs in a bowl.

3 Stir the olive oil, mustard, pepper and balsamic vinegar into the herbs. Season with salt and pepper to taste.

BREAD SAUCE

Ingredients

1 onion

2 cloves

1 fresh bay leaf

1²⁄₃ cups / 400 ml milk

4 oz / 100 g white bread, crusts removed

2 tbsp butter

2 tbsp crème fraîche

Salt and freshly ground pepper

Nutmeg

2 fresh bay leaves, for garnishing

Method

Prep and cook time: 40 min

1 Peel the onion and stud it with the cloves.

2 Put the onion, milk and bay leaf in a saucepan and bring to a boil. Simmer very gently for about 15 minutes.

3 Remove the onion and the bay leaf.

4 Crumble the bread into the milk. Remove from the heat and allow to soak for 15 minutes.

5 Stir in the butter and crème fraîche. Add salt, pepper and nutmeg to taste.

6 Fill a bowl with the sauce. Serve sprinkled with nutmeg and garnished with the bay leaves.

CLASSIC PESTO

Ingredients

½ cup / 50 g pine nuts

3 cups / 60 g fresh basil

2 garlic cloves, peeled

About 7 tbsp / 100 ml olive oil

Generous ½ cup / 50 g grated
Parmesan cheese

Salt and freshly ground pepper

Method

Prep and cook time: 15 min

1 Toast the pine nuts in a dry pan until lightly
browned.

2 Put the pine nuts, basil and garlic cloves in a food
processor. Add half the oil and finely purée.

3 Add the cheese and purée briefly.

4 Mix in enough of the remaining oil to make
a creamy pesto. Season with salt and pepper to taste.

5 Pour into a jar and cover with a thin layer of olive
oil. Close well. The sauce will keep for at least 3 days
if refrigerated.

TOMATO SALSA

Ingredients

6 tomatoes

1 red onion

2 scallions (spring onions), green parts only

3 tbsp olive oil

Salt

Sugar

Lemon juice

Cayenne pepper

Corn chips, to serve

Method

Prep and cook time: 15 min

1 Rinse, quarter and remove the seeds from the tomato and dice the flesh.

2 Peel and chop the onion. Rinse and slice the scallion (spring onion) greens diagonally into thin rings.

3 Mix the tomatoes, onion, scallions and olive oil together.

4 Season to taste with salt, sugar, lemon juice and cayenne pepper. Serve with corn chips.

CRANBERRY AND PISTACHIO SAUCE

Ingredients

2 onions

3 cups / 300 g cranberries

2 tbsp vegetable oil

1 cup / 200 g canned tomatoes, chopped

$2/3$ cup / 150 ml red wine

$2/3$ cup / 100 g pistachio nuts

Brown sugar

Salt

Cayenne pepper

Method

Prep and cook time: 40 min

1 Peel and coarsely chop the onions. Rinse and drain the cranberries.

2 Sauté the onions in a little hot oil.

3 Mix in the cranberries and tomatoes and pour in the red wine. Coarsely chop the pistachios and add them to the mixture.

4 Simmer the sauce, stirring occasionally, for about 30 minutes.

5 Season to taste with the sugar, salt and cayenne pepper.

GREEN MOJO SAUCE

Ingredients

1 cup / 20 g cilantro (fresh coriander)

1 cup / 20 g fresh parsley

1 shallot

2 garlic cloves

About $^1/_3$ cup / 80 ml olive oil

Lemon juice

Salt and pepper

Method

Prep and cook time: 15 min

1 Remove the cilantro (coriander) and parsley leaves from the stems. Peel the shallot and the garlic.

2 Finely purée the herbs, shallot and garlic cloves with the olive oil in a food processor.

3 Season to taste with salt and pepper. Use a a dip with white crusty bread.

THAI SOY DIP

Ingredients

4 scallions (spring onions)

2 garlic cloves

2 red chili peppers

1 tsp fresh ginger, peeled and grated

1¼ cups / 300 ml soy sauce

2 tbsp sesame oil

1 tbsp honey

Method

Prep and cook time: 10 min

1 Rinse and slice the scallions (spring onions) into long, very narrow strips (about 1 inch / 3 cm).

2 Peel and finely chop the garlic cloves.

3 Cut the chili peppers in half. Remove the seeds and ribs and slice into strips.

4 Mix together the peppers, scallions, garlic, ginger, soy sauce, oil and honey.

SWEET CHILI AND GINGER SAUCE

Ingredients

4 red chili peppers

2 cloves garlic, peeled and minced

Walnut sized piece fresh ginger, peeled and grated

½ cup / 125 ml water

7 tbsp / 100 ml rice vinegar, or white wine vinegar

1½ cups / 300 g sugar

½ tsp salt

Method

Prep and cook time: 40 min

1 Rinse the chili peppers, remove most of the seeds and chop the flesh very finely.

2 Put all the ingredients into a pan and bring to a boil.

3 Cook gently for approx 30 minutes, stirring frequently, until the sauce is thick and glossy.

CITRUS DRESSING

Ingredients

1 lime

1 orange

10 tsp / 50 ml sour cream

2/3 cup / 150 g yogurt

About 1 tsp brown sugar

Salt

Mint leaves, for garnishing

Method

Prep and cook time: 10 min

1 Remove the zest from the lime and the orange. Blanch briefly in hot water. Refresh and drain.

2 Squeeze the juice from the fruit.

3 Stir the juice, two thirds of the zest, the sour cream, yogurt and sugar (to taste) until smooth. Season to taste with salt and put into a bowl.

4 Garnish with the reserved zest and mint. This is an excellent dressing for Waldorf salad.

MINT RELISH

Ingredients
For 4 x 1 cup / 250 g jars

1 shallot

5 cups / 120 g fresh mint leaves

½ cup / 125 ml boiling water

1½ cups / 375 ml apple wine

3 tbsp lemon juice

¼ cup / 60 ml mint liqueur

1½ lb / 650 g sugar

Method
Prep and cook time: 1 hour

1 Peel and finely chop the shallot.

2 Discard any damaged mint leaves. Rinse. Reserve one third of the leaves.

3 Combine the other two thirds of the mint leaves with the shallot and the water. Allow to steep for about 15 minutes.

4 Chop the reserved mint leaves and put them in the prepared jars*.

5 Strain the onion-mint "tea" through a sieve. Put the strained liquid, apple wine, lemon juice and sugar in a pan. Bring to a rolling boil and cook for 40 minutes, stirring occasionally.

6 Remove the pan from the heat and stir in the mint liqueur.

7 Immediately fill the jars with the hot liquid. Close tightly and turn upside down for about 10 minutes, until the relish has cooled slightly. Turn upright and allow to cool to room temperature.

* To prepare the jars: Wash and rinse the jars thoroughly with hot water then place in a roasting pan in a 350° F (180° C / Gas Mark 4) oven for 5 minutes to sterilize. Fill the jars while they are still hot.

BARBECUE MARINADE

Ingredients

1 red chili pepper

6 tbsp soy sauce

2 tbsp liquid honey

4 tbsp mild sesame oil

2 tsp finely chopped ginger

1 tsp finely chopped lemon grass

Method

Prep and cook time: 5 min

1 Deseed the chili pepper and slice into rings. Mix together with the soy sauce, honey, oil, ginger and lemon grass.

2 Use to marinate and baste barbecue meats.

PEPPER SAUCE WITH CREAM

Ingredients

1 onion

2 tbsp butter

1 tbsp black peppercorns

2 tbsp flour

Generous ¾ cup / 200 ml beef broth (stock)

7 tbsp / 100 ml whipping cream

2 tbsp green peppercorns, from a jar

Salt

1 tbsp crème fraîche, to serve

Freshly ground pepper

Method
Prep and cook time: 20 min

1 Peel and finely chop the onion. Sauté in hot butter until translucent.

2 Add the coarsely crushed black peppercorns and sauté briefly.

3 Sprinkle in the flour and stir in the beef broth (stock).

4 Add the cream and simmer about 10 minutes, stirring occasionally.

5 To finish, stir in the green peppercorns and season with salt. Serve garnished with a swirl of crème fraîche and some freshly ground pepper.

LEMON, WINE AND FENNEL SEED MARINADE

Ingredients

2 garlic cloves

4 tbsp lemon juice

Scant ¼ cup / 50 ml dry white wine

4 tbsp grapeseed oil

2 sprigs thyme

1 tsp fennel seeds

Method
Prep and cook time: 5 min

1 Peel and slice the garlic.

2 Mix together the garlic, lemon juice, wine, oil, thyme and fennel seeds.

3 Use to marinate and baste steaks or pork.

HARISSA

Ingredients

3 pickled lemons

2 garlic cloves

2 red chili peppers

About ¼ cup / 60 ml olive oil

Salt

Method

Prep and cook time: 15 min

1 Slice the lemons in half and scoop out the flesh.

2 Peel the garlic cloves.

3 Rinse the chili peppers, remove the ribs and seeds if desired.

4 Finely purée the lemon, garlic and chili in a food processor. Add the olive oil in a stream until a creamy paste forms.

5 Season to taste with salt.

SPICY MARINADE

Ingredients

½ tsp coriander seeds

½ tsp peppercorns

½ tsp cumin

1 tsp salt

½ tsp dried thyme

1 tsp paprika powder

2½ tsp sugar

1 tsp chili powder

1 tsp mustard powder

7 tbsp / 100 ml sunflower oil

Method
Prep and cook time: 10 min

1 Coarsely crush the coriander seeds, peppercorns, cumin and salt in a mortar.

2 Combine the crushed spices with the thyme, paprika powder, sugar, chili powder, mustard powder and sunflower oil.

3 Use to marinade and baste steaks, lamb or pork.

ROUILLE

Ingredients

1 slice stale white bread

2 garlic cloves

1 tsp ground saffron

½ tsp salt

1 egg yolk

1 tsp hot mustard

Generous ¾ cup / 200 ml olive oil

1 tsp tomato paste

1 tsp lemon juice

White pepper

Method

Prep and cook time: 15 min

1 Soften the bread in warm water.

2 Peel the garlic. Crush in a mortar together with the saffron and salt.

3 Squeeze the water from the bread very thoroughly. Combine the bread with the garlic mixture.

4 Mix the egg yolk with the mustard.

5 While whisking vigorously, add the oil drop by drop and then in a thin stream to the egg yolk until well incorporated.

6 Stir in the garlic/bread mixture and the tomato paste.

7 Season with the lemon juice and pepper. Serve with fish and seafood soups and stews.

GREEN TOMATO CHUTNEY

Ingredients

For 3 x 2-cup / 500 ml jars

2 lb / 800 g green tomatoes

1 lb / 400 g cooking apples

2 onions

1 tbsp salt

2/3 cup / 100 g raisins

2 cups / 400 g brown sugar

1 cup / 250 ml cider vinegar

2 lemons, juice and zest

1 tsp coriander seeds

1 tsp peppercorns

1 tsp allspice berries

4 cloves

½ cinnamon stick

3 red chili peppers, deseeded and finely chopped

2 tbsp mustard seeds

Method

Prep and cook time: 1 hour 15 min

1 Rinse the tomatoes and cut out the stems. Coarsely chop. Peel and quarter the apples. Remove the cores and coarsely chop. Peel and chop the onions.

2 Put the tomatoes, apples, onions and salt in a saucepan and slowly bring to a boil.

3 Add the raisins, sugar, vinegar, lemon juice and zest to the tomatoes and stir until the sugar has dissolved.

4 Put the coriander seeds, peppercorns, allspice, cloves and cinnamon in a large square of cheesecloth or muslin and bring the edges together, tied with string, to make a bag.

5 Add the spice bag to the pan and simmer, stirring occasionally, for about 30 minutes until the chutney has thickened.

6 Stir in the mustard seeds and chili peppers and remove the spice bag.

7 Fill the prepared jars* with the chutney and close tightly. Allow to cool. Store for at least two weeks before using. The chutney will keep for at least 3 months.

* To prepare the jars: Wash and rinse the jars thoroughly with hot water then place in a roasting pan in a 350° F (180° C/ Gas Mark 4) oven for 5 minutes to sterilize. Fill the jars while they are still hot.

COCKTAIL SAUCE

Ingredients

$^2/_3$ cup / 150 g mayonnaise

3 tbsp ketchup

1 tsp horseradish sauce

Lemon juice

Worcestershire sauce

Salt

Cayenne pepper

1 tbsp chives, to garnish

Method

Prep and cook time: 10 min

1 Mix together the mayonnaise, ketchup and horseradish until smooth.

2 Season to taste with the lemon juice, Worcestershire sauce and cayenne pepper.

3 Garnish with the chives and serve as a dip with the shrimps.

AVOCADO DIP

Ingredients

1 shallot

2 ripe avocados

1 lime

1 tbsp fresh, chopped cilantro (fresh coriander)

Salt and freshly ground black pepper

Cayenne pepper

1 tbsp chives, to garnish

Method

Prep and cook time: 10 min

1 Peel and finely chop the shallot.

2 Slice the avocados in half. Remove the pits (stones) and scoop out the flesh.

3 Cut the lime in half and squeeze out the juice.

4 Purée the avocados with the juice and cilantro (coriander) until smooth.

5 Stir in the shallot. Season to taste with salt, pepper and cayenne pepper. Garnish with the chives and a little cayenne pepper.

TOMATO AND OREGANO VINAIGRETTE

Ingredients

¾ cup / 150 g canned tomatoes, chopped

4 tbsp white wine vinegar

1 tsp honey

6 tbsp olive oil

4 sprigs oregano

Salt

Cayenne pepper

Method

Prep and cook time: 10 min

1 Mix together the tomatoes, vinegar, honey, 2–3 tbsp of water and the olive oil.

2 Remove the oregano leaves from the stems. Reserve a few for garnishing. Finely chop the rest and mix in with the vinaigrette.

3 Season to taste with salt and cayenne pepper. Garnish with the reserved oregano leaves.

APPLE SAUCE

Ingredients

2 lb / 800 g cooking apples

Generous ¾ cup / 200 ml apple juice

1 stick cinnamon

½ cup / 100 g sugar

½ lemon, zest and juice

Method

Prep and cook time: 20 min

1 Peel and remove the cores from the apples and coarsely chop the fruit.

2 Bring the apple juice, cinnamon stick, sugar, lemon zest and juice to a boil in a saucepan. Simmer briefly.

3 Add the apple pieces and cook until the apples are soft and break down (about 10 minutes).

4 Remove the cinnamon stick and allow the sauce to cool.

PARMESAN SAUCE

Ingredients

$^2/_3$ cup / 150 ml hot vegetable broth (stock)

3 tbsp white wine vinegar

4 tbsp olive oil

1¼ cups / 100 g freshly grated Parmesan cheese

Method

Prep and cook time: 5 min

1 Mix together the vegetable broth (stock), vinegar, oil and Parmesan cheese.

2 Season to taste with salt and pepper.

PEPPER DIP

Ingredients

3 red bell peppers

1 red chili pepper, deseeded and chopped

1 clove garlic, peeled and roughly chopped

1 cup / 250 g full fat cream cheese

2 tbsp mayonnaise

2 tbsp olive oil

¼ tsp paprika, for garnishing

Rosemary leaves, for garnishing

Red chili pepper, for garnishing

Method

Prep and cook time: 30 min

1 Place the bell peppers under a hot broiler (grill) and broil until the skins start to blacken and blister, turning from time to time. Let cool.

2 Carefully remove the blackened skins and scrape out the seeds.

3 Put the peppers and all the other ingredients into a food processor and blend until smooth; add a little water if the mix is too stiff.

4 Season with salt and pepper and garnish with a few slices of chili pepper, rosemary leaves and a pinch of paprika.

BECHAMEL SAUCE

Ingredients

1 shallot

2 tbsp butter

2 tbsp flour

Generous ¾ cup / 200 ml beef broth (stock)

Generous ¾ cup / 200 ml milk

1 bay leaf

Nutmeg

3 tbsp whipping cream

1 tsp lemon juice

Salt and freshly ground pepper

Method

Prep and cook time: 25 min

1 Peel and finely dice the shallot.

2 Heat the butter in a saucepan until foamy. Add the shallot and sauté until translucent.

3 Stir in the flour. Continue to stir and sauté until the flour begins to lighten in color.

4 Gradually whisk in the broth (stock) and the milk. Add the bay leaf. Season with nutmeg, salt and pepper.

5 Bring the sauce to a boil while stirring. Simmer, stirring occasionally, for about 15 minutes over low heat.

6 Add the cream and lemon juice to taste and season with salt and pepper.

ONION CHUTNEY

Ingredients

About 1 lb / 400 g onions

1 red chili pepper

2 tbsp raisins

½ cup / 125 ml red wine vinegar

½ cup / 125 ml water

2 tbsp honey

Salt

½ tsp curcuma (turmeric)

2 cloves

1 tsp ground allspice

Freshly ground pepper

Method

Prep and cook time: 30 min

1 Peel the onions and cut into slices.

2 Deseed the chili pepper and cut into into rings.

3 Put the onions, chili, raisins, vinegar and water in a pan. Bring to the boil.

4 Stir in the honey, a little salt, the curcuma (turmeric), cloves and allspice. Simmer gently over a medium heat, while stirring, for about 20 minutes.

5 Allow to cool and season with salt and pepper.

SPICY CHILI SAUCE

Ingredients

2 red chili peppers

1 green chili pepper

1 yellow chili pepper

3 garlic cloves

10 tsp / 50 ml rice vinegar

Generous 1/3 cup / 80 g brown sugar

1 tsp salt

1 cup / 250 ml water

Method

Prep and cook time: 30 min

1 Rinse and cut the chili peppers in half. Remove the ribs and seeds and finely chop.

2 Peel the garlic and finely chop.

3 Put the chili peppers, garlic, vinegar, sugar, salt and the water in a saucepan. Simmer for about 15 minutes until the sauce thickens slightly.

AUBERGINE SPREAD

Ingredients

2 large eggplants (aubergines)

1 small onion

3–4 cloves garlic

1 tsp finely chopped parsley

About ½ cup / 125 ml olive oil, plus some for drizzling

Lemon juice

Salt and pepper

Method

Prep and cook time: 45 min

1 Heat the oven to 200°C (400°F / Gas Mark 6).

2 Prick the eggplants (aubergines) several times with a fork. Put them into the hot oven until the skin blisters and wrinkles and the eggplants feel soft (about 20 minutes).

3 Peel and chop the onion and garlic.

4 Skin the eggplants and remove the stalks. Let cool, then roughly chop the flesh and purée finely in a blender with the onion, garlic and parsley.

5 Stir in enough olive oil to produce a creamy paste. Season with salt and pepper and add lemon juice to taste. Spoon into a dish. Cover and chill before serving. Serve the eggplant purée drizzled with olive oil.

Published by Transatlantic Press

First published in 2011

Transatlantic Press
38 Copthorne Road, Croxley Green, Hertfordshire WD3 4AQ

© Transatlantic Press

Images and Recipes by StockFood © The Food Image Agency

Recipes selected by Rene Chan, StockFood

A catalogue record for this book is available from the British Library.

ISBN978-1-907176-47-0

Printed in China